The
Death
Mazurka

THE
DEATH
MAZURKA

POEMS BY

CHARLES
FISHMAN

TEXAS TECH UNIVERSITY PRESS
1989

Printed in the United States of America

This book was hand-set in 12 on 14 Garamond Old Style
and printed on acid-free paper that meets the guidelines for permanence
and durability of the Committee on Production Guidelines
for Book Longevity of the Council on Library Resources. ∞

The zinc cuts for the illustrations were produced
by Graphic Engraving Services of Columbia, Missouri,
from original drawings by Clarence Wolfshohl.

Cover and jacket design by Cameron Poulter.

Library of Congress Cataloging-in-Publication Data

Fishman, Charles M., 1942–
The death mazurka.
I. Title.
PS3556.I8145D44   1989   811'.54   89-5032
ISBN 0-89672-201-5 (alk. paper)
ISBN 0-89672-206-6 (pbk.: alk. paper)

For my grandmothers

Anna Samalin Szyfman (d. 1917)
Celia Markowitz Ades (d. 1935)

Foreword

These poems are beyond sadness and beyond
anger. In their single-mindedness, in their
sheer accumulation, they are terrifying, and
pure. More than anything else, I think of a
grand mosaic—a mile long, two miles long?—
Yet why could not a small wall contain all
that horror?—Yet why not a miniature? It is a
frozen dance, and one finger is pointed to-
wards God, and one toward that other, and a
third towards oneself, one's head perhaps, or
heart. Why not?

Fishman has done the unthinkable. He has
written an entire book about the murder of
the Jews. It is a delicate book, and dramatic
and exciting. And original. Most of all, it is
brave. How he must have agonized over its
doing—Had he the right?—Who was he to
speak?—Would it be seen as arrogance, pre-
sumption, complacency? He has the right.
He did it well. He helps us understand a
little. He redeems us a little.

Gerald Stern

Acknowledgments

My thanks to the editors of the following publications,
in which some of the poems in this book first appeared:
*Agada, Ararat, The Connecticut Review, Midstream,
Poetry East, Shirim, Response.*

"Guide Me from This Safe Harbor" and "A Morning
at Dachau" are reprinted from *Mortal Companions*
(Pleasure Dome Press, 1977). A much briefer version
of "Portrait without a Face" was also included in
that earlier volume.

I am grateful to Judith Johnson (Sherwin) and to
William Heyen for their helpful comments at crucial
points in my structuring of the manuscript.

A sabbatical from SUNY College of Technology at
Farmingdale enabled me to write key portions of the
manuscript, as did fellowships at Boston University
and Yale University granted by the National Endow-
ment for the Humanities.

Finally, I want to thank Clarence Wolfshohl, publisher
of Timberline Press, for designing and printing the
first edition of this book. I am grateful for his
dedication and courage.

And, to a few others, my love and unspoken thanks.

Contents

Foreword   **vii**

I. European Movements

European Movements   3
Jewish Mouths   4
Star   5
The Hatchet Leaps   6
Woodcutter in the Beech Wood   7
For Janusz Korczak   8
A Stop on the Tour   9

II. Landscape after Battle

After Our Birth   13
Innsbruck: On the *Goethe Way*   14
A Morning at Dachau   15
Tracks Vanishing into Sunlight   17
The Liberator   18
Landscape after Battle   19

III. History

For the Yiddish Poets   23
Pomerantz Unburied in His Poems   24
A Camp Song Newly Heard   25
In Black Rain   26
Auschwitz Nocturne   27
The Blackness of Jews   28
Special Report on the Holocaust   29
Guide Me from This Safe Harbor   30
History   31

The Race   32
The Death Mazurka   33

IV. 1944

September 1944   37
We Polish Jews   39

V. Portrait without a Face

Portrait without a Face   45

VI. Epilogue

Weltanschauung   69
Something Floats Up   72
How to Read Holocaust Poems   73

Every dance is a protest against our oppressors.

–Chaim Kaplan

I
European Movements

European Movements

CÓRDOBA to Hamburg   Bordeaux to
Strasbourg   Marseilles to Rome   Bucharest
to Belgrade   Kalisz to Lublin   Vienna to
Kishinev   Cracow to Lvov   Nomads,
why so restless? Did you hear the voice
of Midsummer lightning? All that back-
breaking portage: Granada to Corfu   Genoa
to Salonika, tireless! Always hurrying
from one black patch to another: Cologne
to Bialystok   Prague to Kiev   Lisbon to
Amsterdam   Tallinn to Polotsk: ceaseless
in your translations! Dear malcontents,
unsettled on dark nights under the moon
of horses: Soncino to Posen   Chernigov
to Frankfurt Avignon to Tarnopol   Berdichev
to Worms   Exiles! Black Sea transports
Crimea Express   Zhitomir to Copenhagen
Helsinki to Antwerp   Starodub to Brest
whirling lights clustered at Satmar   in
the galaxy of Warsaw   starstreams   time
travelers on the dead continent   wrapped
in languages   in the Law's endless bindings
Why didn't you stay put in the whale's
belly? Why didn't you pull the white sky
of silence over your heads? Did the golden
bells of Chelmno charm you? the meadow
    flowers
of Majdanek bend their fiery cups? Did you
rise to the black psalteries of Ravensbrück?
Wanderers! such desire for a life of Christian
culture! such anointings with sacred oils,
bathings in blessed waters!

3

Jewish Mouths

DON'T you see, it is the mouth
you fear   not the nose the side curls
                 not the beard

It is the mouth that will not
        be silenced   that shouts
                 accusations
        though stoppered with earth
mouths that have not forgotten
                 mamaloshen
        though languages swallow
                 their tongues
mouths that articulate a history
        of the planet all your Hellenists
        cannot translate into myth
mouths that shape kingdoms   that kiss
                 the fringes

Jewish mouths filled with the gold
                 of Torah
        that know the taste of a rotting
                 otherness
mouths bathed in acid   scalded
        by knowledge of God

Star

SHE made the star too large—
who knew better? Did they enclose
a template with the order? It was
her nature to be generous. And he?
He walked slowly under the new burden.
At work, the others smiled in their sleeves:
The star among us! one wit called him,
and another: *Star of our nativity!*
Later, under a street lamp, darkness
radiating from him. . . . The butcher's door
was shut but a star scrawled on the glass
spoke openly: *Juden! Juden!* On his back,
his own star moved. *Star of Life.*
Star of Death.

The Hatchet Leaps

ON a black road between dark houses
a hatchet leaps into a peasant's callused hands.

The blade hums, vibrates, gleams like polished
    silver,
strains in the thick fists, as if magnetized,
as if the Jew's cowering back somehow draws it.

The Jew and his hurrying wife—they hunch
    toward the river,
toward the single collapsing planked span above
    it,
above the turbulence.

The Ukrainian can barely hold the blade back!

What is this power that pulls him toward that
    quaking
rectangle of flesh dwindling—lurching now—
as if called by a still greater magic?

What does it matter! The hatchet rules here
—already, his clumsy feet have begun to lift . . .

Yes, see, he floats! he flies gracefully,
held by the pulse of the couple's brazen dance.

Woodcutter in the Beech Wood

AS the saw whined the sawyer
yawned. The child was just
a twig–all twigs today–
soft green wood, too easily
split. And the noise!
horrible shrieks when the blade
caught. Hardly a man's work.
But he knew what the saw
could not and kept a sure grip:
reliable. When a twig snapped,
spattering his plastic gloves
(a bright cheerful yellow),
he cursed the offending sap.
All day, he saw to his task.
Visored like a solderer,
he mourned for the thick
limbs, the whole tree.

For Janusz Korczak

IT is a fine murder of landscape,
Korczak Ziolkowski, to persist
against a mountain, to shape
from the torque of epochs
a monument to Crazy Horse;
but to enter the chamber of death
with no tool but your will,
with no power but your rage
to be human—
                    Janusz, to die
with your orphans, one moment
the work of a life! Your choice
carved a space in the air
over Europe that will endure
when Gîza is dust and the Great
Wall is rubble and Michelangelo's
chapel gapes with the true heaven.

A Stop on the Tour

WE were led to the edge
of the wood. From here,
we could see the open ditch,
a kind of gully or river's
dry bed on which the dead
lay like fish. We watched
and watched—it was broad
daylight—but none ventured
nearer. We had been drawn
by news of the death,
the unparalleled numbers.
This was the chance many
had secretly hoped for:
here was the proof.
I myself could *see*.
They lay uncovered . . .
white, mute, tethered
in clusters. I looked on.
Then one of us coughed:
Time was nearly up.

II
Landscape after Battle

After Our Birth

A pile of them. Not six feet.
Not twelve. Higher. No, not
as tall as an oak. Taller.
As if a silo rose from earth
to sky, its walls invisible
but not the stored dead:
the inexhaustible. No door
in to them, nor out. Miles
of silence articulate as veined
marble—a column unarrested
by the clouds. No entry to them,
no portage out, yet the eye
could see the shapeless heave.
All this, the first day's gift.
Endless days ahead.

Innsbruck: On the *Goethe Way*

IN the snowmelt of postwar Austria,
I walk the old road between sanctity
and hysteria, light shattering
below me like an army of glass dolls.
In tow: two dozen snow-cloaked mountains,
a few thousand freshly-painted houses,
and ten million Austrians—deeply hurt,
ironic behind wood. Survivors
of heraldic battles, they salute
with mechanical fervor, hang baskets
of blood-red flowers from beerhall roofs.
Domed above them, the sky is gold-tooth
yellow, fragile as an infant's skull.

A Morning at Dachau

But what would Munich be without its lovely
surroundings, the rolling hills of Dachau in the
northwest. . . .

—Munich guidebook, 1966

IN the cellar under Dachau
we found charts and pictures:
charts of extermination
planned as a wedding
or funeral,
pictures of Hitler
and his precise mustache
and his human mind.
1 chart of camps
and 1 of cities taken
and 1 of profit value
in prisoner utilization

Underneath our feet
dank unused stone,
around us silent walls—
bloodless, bloodless

Underneath our feet
blank silent stone,
around us unused pipes
mute as arteries

*

What touched was water
in the dark tunnels:

15

like the prisoners' urine,
run-off from despair

grief beading pipes
set into cool walls

light fingers resting
on our shoulders

shoes filling small unlit rooms

*

Outside.
30 mass graves tidy as patios

1 late yellow rose
smelling of young girls
who run and make love

Tracks Vanishing into Sunlight

AFTER rain
this world is not
brightened, streaked
with wet light, runnelled
over with iridescence.

Here there are no dropped
golden feathers, no choiring
wingless flights.
                    All remains:
untransmuted. Held down under
ash drifts—history's weather.

The Liberator

WHAT he saw he has not forgotten.
The country that skirted the camp
was drenched with a red light:
light of first leaves   light
of early morning darkness

What he saw he saw. Sprinkled
with quicklime, the image dissolved
swiftly, but his eyes held the white
aurora. There was a faint hiss
when his boot scraped the rim,

a watery crackling
as if something in his wrist
had begun to escape. Thirty-six
years later, his throat constricts,
memory floods his chest: each year,

an aneurysm ready to burst.

Landscape after Battle

for Andrzej Wajda

TO a nocturne accompaniment—
Chopin—they perform *Liberation*.
As they starved to Vivaldi.
As they burned to Bach.

You ask us to remember when a corpse
was esteemed 'incompletely processed'
that could not, of itself, rise
above the ashfields . . . and dance.

Andrzej, you understand the silence
of your poets: self-hate and catechetical
obedience; violent, unassimilable grief.

Life should taste sweet, milk warm
from the nipple, but in your language
it is salt and blood.

You give us a victim to remind us why we
    speak.

Her name is Nina and—offkey—she sings,
and we are moved by her bare legs
and her loose hair, and we are almost
ready to follow . . . *Red leaves*

build soft mounds under the emptying trees

Poland, here is your Jew!
She will swallow the wafer, translucent

as pale skin, and kiss your numb body
—unkosher meat!

And she will draw you out of your Christ-
blazoned prison, until each bloodied finger
wakens from its dream, until your strangled
voice bears witness:

One life is history enough to mourn.

III
History

For the Yiddish Poets

Everything will remember
That I was here.

—Rajzel Zychlinska

EVERYTHING. Hours of
forgetfulness, caressed
by your attentive lover—
death, the tantalizing!
Sabbaths of intimate mourning.
Droplets that burn the sky's
new body.

That you were here, a presence,
will be remembered, as sleep
is remembered in the dazed glimmer
of wakefulness.

Pomerantz Unburied in His Poems

SHAKES the earth from his shoulders
the moist black earth the loam
of Janow   Bits of rotted bark
rootlets of the forest fly up
from his lips

His first sounds are moans, howls—
bones dream a million years before he
mouths vowels and chews on consonants.

*

Now those verbs of the first morning
seem the exotic oils of faith,
belief brought to a boil, racing off
as steam—at last, visible!

Here on earth, he says, all speech
is garbled, save the lover's speech

*

Heart-cries of the *shofar* spark
from his mouth

A Camp Song Newly Heard

ONCE there was Elzunia.
She is dying all alone,
Because her daddy is in Maidanek,
And in Auschwitz her mommy . . .

Elzunia's remains,
scrawled on a card, sewn
into a coat pocket . . .
1943. The rest of her song

is blood, though we know
the tune to sing: "A Spark
Is Twinkling on the Ash Grate."
A spark is glowing

on the page that keeps
Elzunia's words—
a voice long dead is heard,
a ghost from the fire cries

because her mommy in Auschwitz
died, and in Maidanek her daddy,
because she died alone,
because she was Elzunia.

In Black Rain

for Elie Wiesel

SOME nights only leaves talk
Not a spark catches flame
Not a dog barks

It is cold and late—only you walk
street after empty street

Each yellow leaf is a smoldering star:
torn from a million jackets,
not one could be extinguished

Forty years have scattered
but, in black rain, you burn.

Auschwitz Nocturne

THE Jew at 1 AM moves in near silence

Only a jackboot on the gravel jars him
Only a cat walking out of a black field
mewing her lost children
Only the red throne of light descending
from the amethyst crystal stars

The Jew drinks sleep from his neighbor's
pillow

Only the warning lights at the locked gate
freeze him
Only the new-minted postcards: *We await your
arrival*
Only the ghost viols whispering the yellow gas
of Mozart

The Blackness of Jews

IS the white side of darkness,
a dim light from the black
center of the heart: the ark's

covenant with pain, the word's
promise to the tongue—uttered
in forgetfulness. Desire

that can not be satiated: for justice,
retribution, *wholeness* . . . a cry
from the white glare of the stars.

This is for the children
who came to being in darkness,
for the children and for those

who survived to dream again
of children—children from the fire,
children from ash and anger,

from blind and crippled love.

Special Report on the Holocaust

for Rudy Vrba

SIX million Jews did not die
in the Holocaust: one was missing
. . . escaped to hell or heaven,
to nowhere and to nothing, wrapped
in his prayer shawl, in prison
stripes, in flames: escaped
though gassed, mutilated, hanged;
though frozen with starvation
and exhaustion; though tortured
beyond pain.
        Six million did not
die—though robbed of all he had been,
one was saved: the one of memory,
of dream, of continuance, of revenge:
the one destined to bring the Star
to completion . . . one million lives
for each burning prong.

Guide Me from This Safe Harbor

to Aryeh Lyova Eliav

THE heroes of our people are not always law-givers
with densely flowing beards and eyes like panthers
or broad-shouldered Samsons groaning under a stone
pantheon of fear. You, Aryeh, are one who has loved
with a silent attentiveness . . . lion with olive
   branch!
Tonight, I feel your power. I hear the tale of your
   voyage
beyond the Côte d'Azur, your quest for Zion,
your cargo of abused young women,
eight hundred of them, Himmler-given,
swept from ruined Belsen,
meant for a blood-price, for the hope of pardon,
set to dreaming in a battered banana boat, with you
for captain—how you deceived the bureaucrats, eluded
the British, weathered the turbulence . . . at last,
were captured, entombed at Cypress, released again.
These Jewish women lived, mothered children,
bore arms, laid brick, cleared and tilled and planted.
Aryeh, lion-heart, I would be with you: almost a
   heathen
in this rootless land, I have grown soft with bland
   comforts.
Nothing will be risked while I linger. Tonight,
thought of you pulls me from my safe drift
toward the future. Once more I hunger.

History

I came to a field
that seemed no more than field
and moved on the frozen earth
haunted by cries that rose
above silence

The field was less than field:
a crush of soil and stone
left when a sea's withdrawn:
bones of a field   a crust
of reed and leaf   cracked pod
blown seed of darkness

Yet a light held me   And I cried
Field! Let me be field   let me
honor loss   let me see memory's
darkest web

The Race

THE giant walked
always before me
a giant step
and a step
beyond:
he pushed himself
forward with a fierce
energy. I hurried
after, catching
glints—enough
to see by. Yet
I kept falling
behind—he moved
with such persistence!
I ran faster, raced
till I could see
the back of his skull,
the shaved head
luminous.
I tried to speak—
to turn the giant—
but the shreds
of his flesh whipped
back against
my mouth

The Death Mazurka

IT was late—late in the silence—
yet a mangled tune still rose
as if from a needle trapped
in a warped and spinning groove:
an inarticulate moan
fragmented out of sense
but insistent it be known.

Footfalls turned me around:
a troupe of dancers spun
and kicked and dipped as one—
three score minus one,
and that *one* danced alone.
I watched them skip and prance
but followed only her.

And yes, the drum was swift
and kept a lively beat,
and violins sang sweet
then stridently miaoued—
a mocking sliding note.
She alone danced on
uncoupled, incomplete.

But the trumpets shrilled their tongues
and the saxophones crooned deep
and cymbals scoured the night
to a clashing brassy gleam.
How the women's earrings shined!
like sparks from a whirling fire
that never would be ash.

33

Then the men whisked off their hats
and bowed to the slide trombone
as though it sat enshrined.
But still *she* danced alone
at the edge of the wheeling ring:
I could feel the horizon tilt
when she veered close to me.

Then she turned   then I   then the night
blew back forty years:
I stood in a desolate place,
a reservoir of death
—I could kneel anywhere and drink!
Yes, here was the shul in its bones
and here *Judenrein Square*

and here a few scorched teeth
from some martyred, unknown saint.
The sky was a scroll of pain
—each star a sacred name!
I saw through time in that light.
But I turned and blood rained down
and I turned and dipped and drank

and could not take my fill:
I yearned to find *her* there.
And I turned toward darkness again
where dancers in masks like skulls
twirled in smoke and fire,
whirled in fire and smoke.
Now! screamed the violins.

And she was near as my heart
as we clasped each other and turned.
And *Now!* they shrieked. And *Now!*

IV
1944

September 1944

variations on an article by Arnost Lustig

I stood in the gypsy camp
by the high-voltage wires,
around us the bare Polish
plains and forests.
A thin transparent fog
enveloped the ground, the people.
It penetrated the soul.
A purple fire flashed
from the chimneys,
glowing a deeper purple
before turning into black
smoke. Everything stank.
The smoke became a cloud,
and slowly a black rain—
ashes—dropped down.
Like everyone else, I wished
the wind would shift
or the earth reverse its
direction. The ashes had
a bitter taste. They were
not from coal or burnt wood,
rags or paper.
They fell on us—mute, deaf,
relentless ashes, in which
human breath, shrieks and tears
could be felt.
I stood at the concrete fence post
with white porcelain insulators,
taking it all in like
an hallucination.

A tune from Strauss's *Die Fledermaus*
ran through my mind.

---

*based on the translation from the Czech
by Josef Lustig*

We Polish Jews

for Mother in Poland or to Her Dearest Shadow
New York, 1944

1

AND at once I hear a question—From where that *we*?
Somehow it is just, that question: I am asked it
by the Jews, to whom I have explained that I am not
a Jew, and by the Poles, for whom I will always
remain a Jew.

Here is my answer for them all! I am a Pole
because this is the way I like it. It is my business
and I need not explain or justify. I do not have
to divide Poles into those born right and those born
wrong.

At the innermost, the primitive, there I am a Pole!
A Pole because I was born in Poland, because there
I was both happy and unhappy, because there I learned
and sought to unlearn, the way one may attempt
to discover a new method of breathing. Because
from exile it is necessary for me to come back
to Poland, even if elsewhere I were promised heaven.

A Pole because the Polish language was fed to me
from birth, because when the first shock of poetry
came it came in Polish, because what became most
important—this life, this poetry—is unthinkable
in any other language.

A Pole because in Polish I confessed the anxiety
of my first love, in Polish mumbled of her happiness

39

and troubles. A Pole because a birch and a willow
are dearer to me than a palm or a cypress, and because
Chopin and Mickiewicz are dearer than Beethoven
and Shakespeare—dearer for reasons I cannot explain
with logic!

A Pole because from that country I took many faults
and because I hate those faults with a deeper intensity
because they are of my nation. After my death,
may the earth of Poland take me!

2
But I hear voices saying, Fine, but if a Pole, then why
"We Jews"? Here is the answer: *blood*. So it is
another kind of racism? No, on the contrary! Blood
is double: to and from the veins. The first is the juice
of the body; the other, the blood of a slaughtered
people—not Jewish blood, but the blood of Jews . . .

from this, the deepest and broadest brooks, from this,
a stormy, foaming river. And in this New Jordan I
take my bath: a bloody, hot, tormented brotherhood
with the Jews. *Take me in, my brothers! It is to this
community, to this church, that I wish to belong!*

3
In Warsaw and every other Polish city, there will
remain fragments in permanent and untouched form.
They will be found, these embers of destruction!
And these we will surround with chains, chains forged
from the scraps of Hitler's army.

To the Church of National Memoriams shall be added
another: this sanctuary. Let it be encased in glass
and let an eternal flame flicker at its heart.

40

Only then, when citizens cross themselves near that
shrine, when they kneel before that imagined heat,
will we carry the mark of the Polish Jew—only then,
in pride and mourning, all other ranks diminished.

4
We who—by miracle or by accident—remain alive,
who breathe contrition and shame in the aftermath
of your glory, Redeemers! We—no, not "we Jews,"
but we apparitions, we the shadows of our murdered
sisters and brothers—Polish Jews. We Polish Jews, we
return home now, preserved in our perished bodies.
We return, we arise from the ruins of Europe.

We apparitions! We Schloimes and Shmuels and Moishes,
whose names are adorned now with the shawl
of a revived dignity: our exploits in the catacombs
and sewers, our burials and resurrections—your soap
will never wash out the stains of our blood!

We apparitions! We walk now in the ruins of our stolen
houses, we rise from the bunkers wearing our
murdered names—we soldiers of freedom and honor.
We, for whom every threshold was a fortress. We
crawled toward death, begging for air and choking
on your mercy, but now we take back our skulls, now
our fingers unclasp, and we announce to you our pain:
a scream so fierce and long the furthest generation
shall hear it.

We horrors, we the uncreated, we *Schreckenskammer*.
We apparitions who a new Barnum can present
to the world: *Polish Jews! The biggest sensation! Nervous
people, please leave the hall!*

41

5

I call your name O God from a scatter of graves,
from the graves our children seeded in the body
of Poland. You seed thrower, how far, how thickly
you scattered us!

And now, over Europe, this giant and ghastly skeleton
—in his eyes a violent fire rages, his fingers
tightened in a bony fist. We Polish Jews and he,
our Führer and Savior, who will dictate our rights
and desires!

———————

*reimagined from the Polish of Julian Tuwim
(with Doris Kemp)*

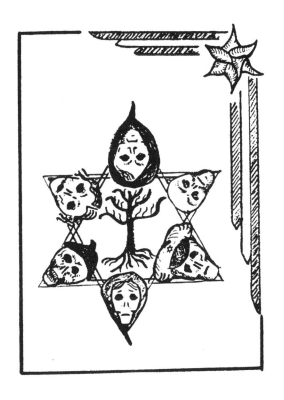

V
Portrait without a Face

Portrait without a Face

for Jack Fishman,
slain by members of the American
Nazi Bund—Quarry Pond, Cortlandt,
New York, August 17, 1935

Those who are alive receive a mandate from
those who are silent forever.
                              —Czeslaw Milosz

1. AN OLD TREE

DEATH cracks his knuckles
in my mind—
I can't teach him
to behave

If I slap his fingers
he points to your grave

Death is a monk
who doesn't sleep

When I snuff out his candle
he puts up neon signs

Death watches
and dreams out loud

*

You were a lady's man
they say,

a confirmed roué
with 3 addresses
and no home

You were a radical Jew
Red Russia's Jew
Jew of the Promise
America's faceless prophet

You fought the Bund
and nailed the lid
on your casket

*

Did you believe in Death?
Death Absolute?

Is that what you risked?

That weekend they woke
from a two-decade rest:
tanks in Watertown
in Cortlandt

Uniforms starched

The brown shirts marched
and drilled till dusk

You headed north
to kick in their drum

Did you see Death come
goosestepping
toward you

with jackboots on?

*

Had you lived
to soldier
in the War,
seen Hitler burned,
I would have heard
your name
before I learned
my own

A photo of your grave,
a star scratched
on a board,
Jack in uniform,
Jack's gun—
I would have stored these
in my brain
instead of toys

*

Are scars hieroglyphs?
And do wounds speak?
And do we grow
a language
with new skin?
And do we wear
the epic poem
of grief?

Must we go blind
to let our fingers read?

Yakov!
do I wear the atoms
of your face?

                    *

I walked away
from life—
wounded stupidly,
scared of love
and death

Found myself deep
behind the lines
in a leafy grove
almost quiet enough
for thought

The blood at my scalp
had dried
and a bird sang
where the fields were smoke
under a red sky

It was a clear song
that heralded nothing
but time,
the pain of things
changing

                    *

I woke into a calm
blackness—
not a star—
no growls of challenge

48

no cannon fire
no war

I was inside
a place so pure
only the smell of earth
came near

And the blue spume
of a past life
filling the void

Yakov! Uncle!
I heard your voice!

Ignorant poet!
Did you think death
was a game?

I a butterfly
and you a cat?

Did you think
you could claw the powder
from my wings?

Did you think
death could be licked
from your fur?

*

Light returned

The bird sang
above my head

and the wound
ached
under my hand

The sun burned
like a face on fire

I wept for your touch

*

Lovers in the park
touch—
an oiled thigh,
a half uncovered breast—
enough

*

I sit under an old tree
and watch:

This tree in summer
holds winter
in its branches—
a nest full of snow
that refuses to melt

In winter it is a tree
only—
when all is bare,
ghostly,
equally lost
against a stilled landscape

When snow jackets
all things
in a deceitful, lavish
sameness . . .

Now, though—
in the lush, clustered,
green-yellow shadings
and patches
of summer—
this tree drinks life
from all directions,
refuses to die
for a month or a moment

Tree,
I have seen time
clinging
like a scarlet dew
to your crown
of branches

*

Yakov!
I begin to see you:

I find your memories
twining about roots
and coiling upwards,
darkening
with thick green foliage

Your shoulders are
strong enough
to climb on,

your hands broad enough
to nest in

And your loves
bloom in the humid musk
of August
like goldenrod
and squash blossoms
and marigolds

Only your face
holds back
in the frosts of winter

Yakov!
show me your face!

*

The sweeping arch
of a branch
upwards   breaks:
a few splinters
lodge in my hair

2. THE BANNER

A light swings, lit,
in a brick building—
sways in the gusts
of steam boiling up
from the dark street

Four men lean
over a card table,

caps pulled low:
they smoke fear down
to the butt

Here is the plan . . .
shivs and slogans

It'll be a picnic!

*

More like a fair:

Young women in drab skirts,
ideals in their hair—
a few in kerchiefs,
the hems of their stockings
straight

They climb briskly
on legs conditioned
by bread lines
—they refuse to lean
on the men

The men push theories
up grassy embankments

A flask head gleams
—a glass eye—
above the stitching
in a back pocket

A pistol pushes
like a cold metal cock
under a khaki jacket

In back of the trees
beliefs are staked
to the ground
like prisoners

One huge gray tent
warps
in the updraft:
the hide of a flayed
elephant

Each tent flap glows
with a swastika
red as chicken blood

The hard earth
glitters,
bits of glassy mica
in its jaws

A sentry walks stiffly
like a bar mitzvah boy

Below me, the pond flashes
in the August sunlight,
treacherous
and inviting

I swim through the slough
of decades

Dead fingers
tug me under

You will not be taken!

Your blood will not
be used
to call the old gods
back

The year's death
hurries in your chest
—a last swift falcon

You are up ahead
in the front ranks:
you carry the banner

Leaves catch flame
as you walk

*

WORKERS OF THE WORLD!

You carry the banner
You get to the gray tent
first—your knife goes in
smoothly
like a scalpel

On his soapbox
the *Kommandeur*
growls and frets
like a jackal

Heil Hitler!
he sputters

You crawl on your belly
but then leap up:

he goes down
into a sunburst

*

WORKERS OF THE WORLD!

Bury your differences

Help swing this hammer:
shatter Deutschland

Who slays *den Führer*
gains repose

Here, comrade,
burn this ancient cross

*

I catch your fingers
in my poem

Jack!
how can I paint
that history?

I have only fragments

A thumb-nail sketch

*

What was death
to you
that you loved her

56

more than life?

When did she propose?

I refuse to acknowledge
your vows . . .

I want you back!

*

I walk down
your old turf:
half-demolished buildings
scaffolding
pigeons flying
through chimney necks
bricks blackening
under the moon's
acid touch

Radios on the pavement
squawking *You're next!*
Ph.D.'s hawking hotdogs
old men in cribs
old women hunting
survival
in trash bins

Through broken panes
I watch the light
sway—

Your bones will not stay
buried

I can hear your voice lift
over the night's backed traffic

I climb into this dark room—
it is brighter in here
than outside

*

You are the lost limb
of the amputee:
when it rains
the ghost-nerves scream

If I press my ear
to the earth
I can hear a train
chuffing
on iron tracks

If I lie flat
I can hear
children mewling
like baby seals,
women squealing,
old men in wheezy
prayer

If I lie flat,
face downwards,
I can hear the time-
bomb
ticking in each car

*

Yakov!
I want you back!

3. A DOG LICKS MY FACE

A dog licks my face,
his tongue scours
and chastens

I want to come up
for air
but I can't find
my feet,
I can't touch bottom

*

You told me nothing,
father,
nothing of life
and pain—
did you think I
should suffer
your mistakes
again?

Is this tradition?

What of Jacob?
What of your lost brother?

Couldn't you see
I would guess
a ghost lived
with us?

*

In a large field
a man runs,
a dog follows:
they chase each other
into the dark

The wind blows rain
gray as a uniform
blackening into death

And the tree
is crown-less:
it pushes up
into the eye socket
of the storm

You come, spider,
down the life-line
of time

*

Crawl under my hair

Tell me of your nights
behind curtained windows,
your life radiant—
drawing the hot current
of the age—
adorning you
like a chrysalis
ready to burst

Tell me of the nights

at the edge:
a green field before you
and the urge to run

And the dome of light
at the barricades

Tell me, Spirit Father,
who is this woman
who wears your body
like her skin?

And this man, your comrade,
what does he keep
of you?

Crawl deeper,
do you see this old wound?

Narrow passage . . .

Come!

*

The curtains blow back
into your room:

Where is the switch
that turns vision on?

*

Skull uncle,
bone father

We walk mind in mind
burning off the haze

The ground beneath us
a phosphorescent maze

Only your hand on me burns

We walk on slick stones

I see the gun blaze
with noon sun . . .

You quarry of images!

*

Broken glass on concrete
voices
unintelligible congregations
behind lit windows

Barbed wire between apartments:
encampments

Red patches on brown shirts

A steady hum
that shortcircuits everything

*

I paint a yellow star
upon your grave,
clear the rubble

I paint at night
working carefully

A dog licks my face
and spills the paint:
enough remains on the brush,
on my fingers

*

A loudspeaker
tracks me down,
announces your doom:
asphyxiation
through drowning,
grappling hooks,
negligence,
communism,
careless hands,
anger,
crushed ribs,
protruding rocks,
skull fractures,
confusion,
fascism,
meetings
in strange rooms

Your blood will not wash
from these quarry stones

*

Yakov!
it is on my face

My children wear your star,
sulk in your catacombs,
tunnel beneath the bones
of six million

They wear your star
like an ornament—
how long before they feel
it burn?

Yakov!
it is on my face!

*

The sun struggles to appear
at midnight

Did you think I
had forgotten?

Your spirit's son?

I call you back . . .

Raise my neck hairs,
make the blood come
throbbing
against my body

*

6 million—
I can not ever
see them

There are too many wings
struggling to break free

Dying again
and rising
and, again, dying

But you,
flying against the wind
of my vision,
your wings settle
on my lips
like shrouds

*

Yakov!

Seek some way in!

It is dark here,
and darkly silent

I will not look
to see your face again

I will not look for you
again
under this dead tree
that burns green
in the rain

VI
Epilogue

Weltanschauung

Where is the lightning to lick you
with its tongue? Where is the frenzy
with which you should be inoculated?
                    —Nietzsche

THE *Sieg! Heil!* Victory! Salvation!
jackboots out the last flame of reason.

The lightning comes later: the blazing
arms of the sun twisted clockwise
toward pain, glittering on the dial:
little flares—each with its face,
its annihilation.

                    *

You refused to believe the bearded
faces, eyes that had seen into the nerve-
ends of civilization, had seen Kafka
shrivel in that holocaust, Einstein
reduced to a small cupful of ash.

Blond hair curled in the bookish heat.
Blue eyes cheered to see Marx char.
Freud blistered and blackened and cracked
like a burnt up child.

                    *

In the *shtetls* chess tables filled
with cooked fish. Prayer shawls grumbled
with fire in the wooden *shuls*. *Kristallnacht*

knocked the teeth from your skulls.

The vault clicked shut and Churchill
sipped his tea. You wore the star
and time would make you free.

*

Death wagons gouged through the ghetto
like a rich man's purse.

Each Yid was corpse and hearse.

*

You were artisans, poets, actors, teachers,
coopers, cut-throats, dreamers, debaters.

You loved, hated, feared death, feared failure.
You lied to yourselves, to God, to each other.

You had nowhere to go, yet a train waited.

*

No food. No water. No air.
Wheels whacked against your feet
like rifle butts.

When they unbolted the car you stared
through the Butcher's door.

*

Himmelstrasse: the last tick of the clock.

70

And you moaned, and you cried out.
And you went singing, and you choked
on courage.

And God was there, and there was nothing.

*

In winter, ashes from the crematoria
were spread like a gray smudge
over the frozen roads.

Something Floats Up

at the warehouse for salvaged
Yiddish books

SOMETHING floats up from memory
too powerful for words:
these are the books of the vanished
Jewish people—their sisters
went up in flames.

Each is a map that can not be
translated, a fragment that speaks
to fragments

a live swan that flutters against
our mouths

How to Read Holocaust Poems

THE sun beats down
its cryptic ode
to violence
and desire rides high
in the saddle
of the cold wind:
tufts and drifts
of straw,
slivers of soap
and charred bone.

Forgiveness is not
the theme
nor is despair.
Only the first hush
matters—
the rest, a voice that
drones
at a deaf ear.

Though each verse
rings true,
the poem is a lie:
only one's ache
to speak
matters—
only one's hunger
to waken.